Content
is <u>still</u>
KING
by
Lisa Sutherland

Table of Contents:

A New Era of Online Marketing

2017 is a wonderful year for online business. The sky is the limit with online business and 2017 has an online economy that's filled with opportunity. According to the IAB, advertising revenues hit $32.7 billion dollars in the first half of 2016 in the United States alone. This completely disregards unpaid revenue that has been generated throughout the year.

Today, it may feel like you're at a competitive disadvantage when it comes to building a successful online business. Luckily, with a little bit of conscious effort and sound strategy, anyone can build an online business that will thrive for years to come.

2017 is the year where anyone can succeed through sound strategy and hard work. You don't need to hire a team to get started and anyone can start a successful business. Qualifications and advertising budgets can be useful, but they can also be thrown out the window while a new business owner establishes his or her website.

All it take is to start making money is a live website, a passion for your business and the ability to understand how the industry works. Through using simple but effective strategies, you'll begin to understand online business as a machine that works for you while you're away.

There will never be any substitute for hard work, but it's nice to have a business that stills operates after you clock out for the day.

The main principles in this book is the basic recipe for setting up an effective website with zero coding experience and for as little as $20.

After you your online business, you'll be introduced into the style of businesses you can run. After you set up your market, you'll be presented with strategies for effectively understanding your market and to tap into the market so you can try to generate your first sale.

Anyone during the golden era of online business can become successful.

It takes using simplistic but proven tactics to build the foundations of your new online business. However, with a little bit of patience, you'll be able to build your own business from scratch.

Out with the days where it takes months of hard work and 10s of thousands of dollars to start a business. In with the days where you have the chance to build a multiple million dollar business through only investing your time and a hundred bucks to get started.

Working for an online business is fun and if done properly can become transform your income. Welcome to the wonderful web and remember that the only way to succeed is through action. This book is a simplistic but successful way to get your business off the ground. If you apply this book, you'll successfully have a website launched and you'll have built the crucial mechanics of an online business that works.

Chapter 1: Follow This Formula to Discover Profitable Online Markets

Finding A Market That Works For You:

The first major aspect about starting your own online business is something that draws a large portion of middle class workers into the business.

It is the prospect of starting a business through making one of your passions your job. It may seem impractical at first, but learning how to work on a business you truly enjoy will allow you to succeed in the long run.

Step 1 to Selecting Your Business:

When you're trying to discover your passion, what you want to do may come easy . However, without properly diving into your deeper emotions, you'll find yourself lacking the appropriate drivers to succeed as you launch your online business.

There are 3 main methods to allow you to identify a passion.

1. Ask yourself a series of questions.
2. Freewrite about what online business you'd like to launch.
3. Build your list.

Method 1: A Series Of Questions.

Asking a question is believed by many experts to be the most powerful way to unearth your inner emotions and unlock your passions.

It allows you to contemplate perspectives about life that you may not have addressed for years and will remind you of what's most important to you and your life.

This method will allow you to utilize those hidden gems that can drive you through success and will remind you exactly why you want to start a successful online business .

Here are 25 Questions that will spark powerful emotions inside of you and will help steer you in the right direction as you select which market you'd like to start your first online business.

In order for this exercise to be most successful, set a timer for 5 minutes and continuiously write each question through

1.   **What makes you feel fulfilled?**

2.   **What do you find enjoyable?**

3.   **If you money was not an object of importance, what would you do with your life?**

4.   **What would you like to be remembered for 15 years from now?**

5.   **When you die, what would you liked to be remembered for?**

6.   **What skills do you have that contribute to your favorite pastimes?**

7.   **How much time do you spend doing things you don't enjoy?**

8.   **How much time do you spend doing things that you do enjoy?**

9.   **What are your core values in life?**

10. **How much of your life do you spend displaying these core values?**

11.   What values and passions are you currently ignoring?

12.   In your life, what are you sacrificing for income?

13.   Do you have any fears that are stopping you from pursuing your dreams?

14.   What would your perfect day look like?

15.   What is the smallest salary you can earn to pay your bills?

16.   What is the worst thing that could happen if you tried to pursue launching an online business while you earn you current income?

17.   How has not pursuing your dreams impacted your life?

18.   If you continue to accept your current conditions, how would you feel about your life as you gear up for retirement?

19.   If you pursue your dreams and failed, how would you feel about your life gearing up to retirement?

20. If you pursue your dreams and succeeded, how would you feel about you life gearing up to retirement?

21. Do you have a bucket list?

22. How far have you come in completing your bucket list?

23. How would your life transform if you started a business that you loved?

24. How would you live your life if you had no financial boundaries?

25. How would your quality of life improve if you made money doing what you love?

Spend 2 Minutes answering every question through constant writing.

You don't have to stop at 2 minutes but it is important to express your reaction to each question for a couple minutes.

This will build an identification of what's important inside of your life. It's easy to get wrapped up with our day to day life and to accept it.

By contemplating what life holds if you make money doing what you love, you'll begin to discover the power that starting an online business has inside of your life .

How do you use these answers to begin selecting a market that will be profitable for you?

It's important to understand what drives you for a better life and what makes you happy, but it's also just as crucial to understand the impact that a job which doesn't make you feel complete has.

These questions will open up the contemplation on how you would like to spend your life? You'll begin to see what really inspires you inside of life. By using these questions to unlock how you'd truly love to spend your life, you'll begin to shift your attention towards what matters.

WRITE DOWN YOUR BIGGEST 5-10 TAKEAWAYS YOU GOT FROM ANSWERING YOUR QUESTIONS.

Don't discredit the things you love and always try to stay true to your core values.

These questions were designed for you to understand how important it is to spend your time on Earth by staying true to yourself. When you're looking to build an online business, it means that you're looking for an increased quality of life.

Through identifying what you're looking for, you'll be able to fine tune the process of transitioning careers and you'll begin to work towards this opportunity to develop a lifestyle that's good for you.

Be willing to invest blood sweat and tears as you start your online business.

It would be wonderful if you could just wake up, tap a couple buttons and start a business.

But unlike most of the flashy online business advertisements, it takes some dedication.

While you start a business, you'll inevitably encounter a surge of resistance. It can come in various forms. Your family, your friends, having fun, your internal struggles, your doubts, and even relaxing.

The only way for you to succeed in creating a business is through leveraging your free time. If you associate creating a business as more important than sustaining your current life, you'll succeed. However, if your current life takes over your free time, you'll consistently put your online business on the back burner.

Short term sacrifice is very common when your building a better life over the long term. By being able to leverage your emotions in favor of building a business, you'll take the necessary action to start a business.

Remember how long life is.

If you spend 75 years on this planet, you'll have the blessing of living a total of 27,375 days. If you work hard for 600 days to build a more incredible life, you'll only have to spend 2% of your life building a business that will change your life forever.

What it comes down to is how much of your life are you willing to spend doing something frustrating when it only takes a little investment to have more enjoyment for the rest of your life?

You may recognize that the truly important things in life are pretty simple: work that's engaging and feels meaningful, family and friends who care about you, experiences that fulfill and enliven you, and a home that's safe and comfortable.

Enjoying the process is more important in business than where your journey ends.

A pivotal part of success in online business is working on a business that you're passionate about. By enjoying setting up your business, you'll be able to count the time you spend working as entertainment. Luckily, after a couple of months of grinding away, you'll find that you begin getting paid for what you enjoy doing and you'll be able to make a push at replacing your job.

If you take this approach, your work at building a business won't feel like work and by the time you have enough money to pay the bills, you'll realize that your job is a thousand times better than your old work.

What's better than that? Well you get to do what you enjoy anywhere in the world and you get to set up your own schedule. That makes it pretty easy to smash out your bucket list like a champion.

Method 2: Freewriting

Freewriting is the second method you will use to discover which market you would like to work in. The objective is simple. Set a timer and write 15 minutes non-stop about what online business you would like to develop.

The rules to free-writing are simple.

Rule 1: Imagine that you've launched a successful online business that you love.

The first rule to successfully identifying your market through free-writing is by imagining that you're already making a healthy income through online business. Feel what it's like and begin to feel what working for yourself brings to the table. As you begin to paint a picture inside of your imagination, all you have to do is from there is to imagine how much fun you're having.

Rule 2: Look at the markets that your business is successful in.

When you're imagining your enjoyment, look at what markets your business is in and what type of products your selling. This will steer you in the write direction and will give you a boost in discovering what type of business you'll be good at running.

Is your business filled with collectibles? Games? Writing? Reading? Fitness? Self-Help? Coding? Entertainment? Technology?

Sports? Cooking? Organization? Interior Design? Parenting?

What are you truly passionate about when it comes to making a bigger impact in both your life and others around the world?

Whatever comes to you for business ideas is perfectly fine. We'll address whether or not you can make money from your ideas in the third method.

Rule 3: Always keep your pen moving no matter what happens.

The most important part about free-writing is tapping into your subconscious mind so that you can develop a nice flow. Through doing this, you'll eliminate over analyzing and open up brainstorming for fun business ideas.

Rule 4: Write as quickly as you can.
Writing as quickly as you can will allow you to get a nice flow inside of your free-writing It stops you from thinking too technically and it takes limiting beliefs out of the picture.

Rule 5: Always use the first word that comes to your mind.

Rule number 5 is just another way to work with your mind to create a nice flow of ideas. While you're writing, you don't have to think of the best way to express an idea. Just document what you have inside of your mind and continue through.

You're going to realize that your biggest insights will come at the back end of your writing. However, this can only happen if you take what you immediately get and document it.

Now set your timer and get writing even if you think you know what you'd like to do. This will allow you to open up new angles for your online business that lie beyond the surface of your initial intentions.

WHAT TO DO WITH YOUR FREEWRITING.

Now that you've completed your 15 minutes of free-writing, it's time to look through it and take out 5-15 gems you discovered from the market.

Document them on a separate page for safe keeping. Ensure that you have 5 takeaways for markets inside of online business. One of them will likely be good enough to make a solid income through.

Method 3: Checking To See if Your Business Is Profitable.

Every idea you have for business may not work for you so it's important that your efforts and commitment to building a better life comes through with income.

There are a lot of ways to check to see if your business will be profitable, but this easy to used method presented below will do the trick in letting you know if the market you'd like to start a business in is profitable.

UNDERSTANDING A PROFITABLE NICHE

Before you launch your online business, it's important to find a niche that is profitable. A niche is a group of people who are interested inside of a certain topic.

Step 1:

A great way to start is through using Google's free keyword marketing tool. Through simply signing up as a marketer, you'll be able to identify keywords that are similar and how much search volume the market gets every month.

Type in about 25 to 50 topics you could engage in for fun and check out the results. After you get a nice list of keywords, you'll be able to get more of a grasp on how many people are actively looking and engaging with solutions and information around your business idea.

Step 2:

Now that you have a nice grasp on how big your market is, it's time to check out if the top websites inside of your markets are profitable.

All you have to do is search Google for the list of keywords you listed out and to copy and paste the top 10 websites into the free version of SEMRush.com. This will give you a nice map of how many visitors the website organically gets through search, the main competitors, and whether or not the company spends money on advertisement.

Also document whether or not advertisements show up on Google and pay attention exactly what they are selling. Back check to see how long the campaign has been running for and how many campaigns the business has run over the course of a couple years.

You'll begin to realize that some ads have been up for months and maybe even years. This indicates that the business and market you're in is certainly profitable. But if you found some businesses that are generating nice income and spending money on ads, the journey only starts here.

Step 3:

Look at how every website tries to make money. Are they trying to capture emails? Do they have a store or products? What type of products are they trying to sell and how much are they selling these products for?

Double check how long the site has been active, but odds are this company has been around for years . During this time, the online business has tested thousands of ways to sell their products, generate readers and make money from their business.

Step 4:

Sign up to every email and look at what they are trying to offer and how they present their statistics. By looking at what the best businesses are talking about, you'll begin to understand the emotional drivers of the market.

Step 5:

Now that you have a nice foundation for topics, products and sales, it's time to look at the profiles and pages that are dominating twitter and facebook. You'll find some companies that thrive in both of the markets, but you'll also learn tons as you shift your attention into social media. Document the top 50 influencers inside of your market and begin to develop

In twitter, you can use a series of tools that are currently free.

http://buzzsumo.com/ is a wonderful place to start. You can get a couple search results with fantastic engagement over the topics that you're looking for. The premium service is $99/month, but the free version is a perfect way to get a feel for how your market is responding to topics.

https://klout.com/home is another website that makes it easy to find the influencers inside of the market that you're trying to start your business. If you have some powerful influencers, document them and begin to follow them on social media platforms. These influencers are incredible about understanding the buzz and emotional triggers of their market. By understanding what they engage in, you'll be able to develop a feel for how your online business can become successful.

By using a combination of search engine and social media powerhouses, you'll learn how much engagement you can develop inside of your market and approximately how much money you can earn on a monthly basis.

MOVING FORWARD:

Now that you have an understand of how many followers and visitors your market engages with, you can determine whether or not you can make an income through business.

Now that you have a good feel for whether or not your business idea is profitable, it's time to move onto the next stage.

A QUICK SHORTCUT & HELP IF YOU'RE NOT SURE EXACTLY WHAT MARKET YOU'D LIKE TO JOIN.

If you're still having trouble with a market to tap into, you can look into a couple websites to help guide you.

Nichehacks has two great pages:
http://nichehacks.com/101-resources-discover-hot-niche-ideas/
http://nichehacks.com/category/niche-market-ideas/

And Eben Pagan has a nice free report mapped out here.
http://getaltitude.com/wp-content/uploads/2014/08/Video_2_Niche_Intelligence_Report.pdf

Chapter 2: The 5 Most Important First Steps in Your Online Business

Setting up your online business can be a little overwhelming if you're not sure where to look. Luckily, this book gives you a couple of different options to set up your online business with no coding experience and for as low as $20-$100.

SETTING UP YOUR WEBSITE:

Setting up your website can quickly turn into a nightmare and can cost thousands of dollars. Luckily, this can be avoided by using simple platforms designed for making starting a business easy.

There are 5 steps to launching your website.

Step 1: Buying a profitable domain.
Step 2: Buying Hosting.
Step 3: Purchasing A Website Theme.
Step 4: Installing Your Website
Step 5: Setting Up Your Website for Visitors.

STEP 1: BUYING A PROFITABLE DOMAIN.

When you're setting out to purchase a domain for your business to run on, you'll quickly discover that a lot of names are taken. However, with a little bit of patience, you'll be able to find a domain that works for you.

There are a lot of domains out there available inside of your market, but it's important to buy the right one. The name of your website is the staple of all of the content you'll be producing over the next couple years. For instance, instantclassiccollectables.com was available at the time of this publication and so was simplydeliciouscooking.com.

When you select a name for your business, there are a couple of guidelines you can follow, but at the end of the day, you want it to become the staple of your business. It's kind of like naming your brand.

Here are a couple of crucial but simple steps to allow you to find a profitable domain inside of your market.

Part 1: Brainstorm A Good Name For Your Blog.

There technically aren't any laws of profitability in selecting a name for your website, but it has to be relevant to the market you're starting your business in. Here a few guidelines to get you started.

Try to blend a keyword into your name.

By using a key topic for your business, you'll be able to develop a memorable website for your potential customers. It gives you the perfect platform to describe what your business is about and more about the nature of your content and solutions. In the examples presented above, the you automatically know what the type of business that website would be. So list off about 20 topics you'd like your website to be known for.

Make your website name easy to remember.

When you score a good connection with a visitor, they don't always convert into business. And without making a name that is memorable, you'll loose that customer forever even if they try to find your website dozens of times.

In order to avoid this, it's good to use a catchy name that connects to your topic. For example, sassybutclassy.net is an available domain name that could be used for high end fashion.

But luxurybrandclothing.com may get lost into the abyss of the luxury brand clothing market. When you score a potential customer through hard work, it's important to get them back as often as you can. The first step in doing this is having a name that's catchy and easy to remember.

Keep your name short and sweet.

Theincrediblesagaofatechnitionsguidetothecl oud.com is a terrible name for a website that's designed for showing small businesses on how they can utilize cloud platforms.

Instead think about using cloudprofits.com. If possible, try to keep the website name under 20 characters. This isn't always a necessity, but the shorter and catchier the name, the better your results will be.

Avoid Hyphens If Possible:
You don't have to kill hyphens, but remember that a lot of your traffic for forex-profits.com would go to forexprofits.com. When you have to use a hyphen in your domain, it's important to understand that you're sharing your brand name with someone else who could hijack all of your hard work. However, if you absolutely love a name, hyphens can help you name your business in a competitive market.

Only use .com, .net and .org.
These 3 extensions are absolutely crucial when sparking authority for your business. A lot of raving has been circling about the new extensions but buying them puts your business at risk of never ranking in google and also diminishes the seriousness of your business.

Make your name fun!

Another great way to name your website is by making it enjoyable and catchy. That is all.

IF YOU'RE STRUGGLING TO COME UP WITH A NAME:

It's pretty common to struggle with names for your website. So in case you're confused as to what really works and what doesn't, you can't look at a "top blogs" list inside of your market. This will give you the opportunity to brainstorm new ways to connect your initial idea and will give you a good idea of what names are popping inside of the topics you'd like to launch your business in.

Part 2: Brainstorming Your Favorite Domain Names

Now that you have a couple of ideas about how to name your website, it's time to brainstorm 15 names for you website.

In order to spark your creativity, you can ask yourself what the key solutions the market needs and as well as the key problems.

If you're still having trouble you can turn to the phonological loop. This is our audible buffer system. As we hear or see a name, it bounces around in the brain for a couple seconds before it's processes. The key in this system is to get the name of your website to register inside of your visitor's brain through expanding the amount of time a name is registered. In order to do this, you can use a series of repetitive sounds.

You can also think of words that rhyme or are rhythmic by nature. Think of a four by four rhythm like you would a top 40 song.

A KEY NOTE. IT'S OK TO SIT ON YOUR NAME FOR A COUPLE OF DAYS. IF YOU DON'T FIND A NAME THAT HITS HOME RIGHT AWAY, IT'S TOTALLY FINE. KEEP PLUGGING AWAY AND LOOK UP CREATIVE METHODS AND NAMES FROM FORTUNE 500 COMPANIES AND FAMOUS WEBSITES. YOUR NAME WILL COME WITH TIME, DON'T WORRY.

Part 3: Seeing if your domain is available

Now that you have a couple of names down, it's time to see if it's available! The perfect website to use when your checking out names for your website would be through using godaddy.com. It has a friendly interface and has fantastic customer support and an easy to use platform.

All you have to do is follow this link and type in what website you'd like to buy. If it's available, purchase it now and get started on building your website! Add on the hosting option as well and you'll be great until you have to upgrade your hosting! If it's not, continue to brainstorm and see if there's other options available. Think of catch phrases or hooks to take your ideas further.

STEP 2: BUY HOSTING

Now that you have a domain, it's time to connect this domain to a server so your website becomes active. When buying hosting, it's best to host your website through godaddy. It will allow you to start off your business but be warned that your website could crash from the servers every once in a while. If you're looking for a different option, you can use this link to PCMag to get your website live.

http://www.pcmag.com/article2/0,2817,242
4725,00.asp

STEP 3: FIND A THEME

Now that you have an active website, it's time to find a theme that will bring your business to life. It's highly recommended to use wordpress. They use templates that you can install on your website with absolutely no experience. When you're cruising around shopping for themes, it's best to understand load time, elegance, and user engagement.

By far the best theme available for customizing your website in a way that is user and Google friendly is a template called Divi.

https://www.elegantthemes.com/blog/theme
-releases/divi-3

It allows you to easily build your website exactly the way you like it even if you have no clue what you're doing. If you're not into building your website from scratch, elegant themes has over 80 themes you can use.

It only costs $70 for a year of access to the themes and is the perfect place to create an unforgettable website for your online business. If you happen to cancel your membership, you can still use your templates. You just can't download updates or new themes in the future.

A more expensive alternative is to use the genius platform from studiopress.

If you don't want to pay for a theme, you can find a free one simply by searching free wordpress themes. However, your website will be branded by the designer. You can also purchase a theme through themeforest.net.

No matter the route you take, it's important to ensure that your website is SEO friendly. And just a quick word of caution. "SEO" templates can suck. However using elegant themes and studiopress will put you in the perfect position to focus on your business rather than worrying about whether or not your customers can actually engage inside of your content and whether you'll ever be visible on Google.

STEP 4: INSTALLING YOUR THEME.

Installing your theme through the godaddy website will be really easy. Here's an article that will allow guide you through the process .
https://www.godaddy.com/help/install-wordpress-834
Then install your theme through this quick and easy guide:
http://www.wpbeginner.com/beginners-guide/how-to-install-a-wordpress-theme/

STEP 5: SETTING UP YOUR SITE FOR GUESTS.

Now that you've finally set up your website and its live, it's time to set up your online business for visitors. You can do this by breaking your website down into a series of categories. A perfect way to set up your website is to build it like the best top 10 blogs on your topic.

What tabs(categories) do they have up on top of the page? How is their homepage laid out? How do they present their content? And what do their article look like? Do they have a blog tab or is their entire business a stream of content? Do they have a store? What do they sell? What parts of the pages are they trying to acquire emails from?

Build a major prototype for you website through already successful businesses. When you develop more into your business, you can rearrange your website however you feel, but for now it's best not to reinvent the wheel if you don't already know how to build a jet.

In the next chapter, you'll learn how to set up your website with pictures how many articles to write and what to write about to get your business ready for customers. But for now, research on the top 10 blogs inside of your market and build a skeleton model for your website.

Set up categories, a basic structure for your front page, a basic model for a sales page, a basic model for acquiring an email, a basic model for each category and a basic structure for each individual articles. By paying attention to these specific aspects of the top 10 businesses, you'll set your website up for a better model of success. This is why the Divi 3 is so powerful as you develop your website, but any theme will do. Just make sure you structure your website using the same model of already successful online businesses.

SETTING UP SOCIAL ACCOUNTS:

There are only two social media sites that you need to use when you start your online business. Twitter and Facebook. These two platforms may not be loved by everyone, but they are important if you'd like to generate free traffic to your online business.

Use the name of your website to create a page for Facebook and an account on twitter.

Here's a solid step by step guide to setting up your account on twitter:

http://aliciaorre.com/social-media-and-digital-marketing/twitter/set-up-twitter-account

Here's how to set up a Facebook page .

https://www.facebook.com/help/104002523024878?helpref=about_content

Chapter 3: How You Create Content That Bring in Profits

Content is the backbone of every successful online business. Today, there are millions of profitable websites that can attest to the power of creating the right content and there's no substitution for the king of the web. The right content can transform a failing business into a thriving one and can allow any new compay to take the spotlight.

Building your content foundation is the perfect to kick off your website and the strategy is incredibly simple. However, making successful content isn't as easy as everyone says. It takes a lot of hard work and understanding to develop content that can create exposure for your business.

Luckily, there's a shortcut.

The second book in this series,titled 2017 Guide For Traffic Through Social, will shed light into the complexities of building incredibly successful content, but for now, we can use a hack that will allow us to get the ball rolling.In the previous chapter, you set up the skeleton of your website through the same categories that the top businesses inside of your topic used.

Now all you have to do is simply model and rewrite the top 5 articles on every category through the search results you get from the free version of buzzsumo.

In the buzzsumo filter, you can look at videos, articles and infographics. You can even look at the articles that were shared most on twitter and facebook.

Through using this free tool, you can find a perfect place to start your business content generation and you'll be able to quickly develop content that's engaging when you attract your first visitors to your online business.

If you'd like, you can even type in the domain name for the top 10 businesses in your topic and look at their highest viewed articles and see where they are positioned inside of the website. This will allow you to develop a sense of what's a suitable topic inside of the market and what you can use to start off your business.

However, it's important to note that some of the buzz may be a result of viral news. Pay attention to when this article was written and how it was marketed in social media.

In total, it's best to have about 30 articles of content to prove that you have a nice grasp inside of the market.

After you develop your first 30 articles with a length anywhere from 500-1,500 word. Ideally, your website should be producing one unique article every day. Before you publish any content, make sure that your article is 100% unique.

You can use copyscape or a free alternative comes from small seo tools. Make sure you post your content to facebook and twitter during the prime hours inside of your market. You'll notice that you get the least views on a Saturday, but you'll also discover that you get the most engagement with your website during the same time. Also, most content gets read around 7AM and less content gets read during the evening than it does during the afternoon.

You'll find a sweetspot with your content. You don't have to over analyze your release times right away but do experiment at what times you release your posts and what happens during these hours .

Now that we have more of a nice view on content, it's time to present the 7 key aspects to developing content that will naturally create more views and engagement.

7 aspects to writing a successful article.

Whether you believe it or not, writing great content will separate whether your business succeeds or fails. It doesn't matter what you're selling and what business model you use.

Creating wonderful content takes hard work and special attention but it's the only way to build your business. If your not in the business to talk about what you love, you can hire some writers, but your sales will slump until you develop a powerful understanding of your market.

Content is known to make you visible on Google, will boost how many people engage with your business and will even lead you to the path of riches before it's all said and done. No matter what business your in, creating great content is a job that must be done the right way.

Here are the 7 aspects of great content.

1. Your content has to be original.

Even though you're writing on a topic that's been already read by thousands of people, it's important to understand that you have to put your own unique twist on all the material you ever write. As mentioned, original content goes a long way with Google and your visitors. Copying other people's words will come back to bite you with time. So put a new perspective to the game and introduce a new twist. It's hard when you first start an onine business to generate fresh content that can make a splash inside of your markets.

However, a few simple questions will let you create content that's original and inspiring for your readers.

When you sit down to create a piece of content from buzzsumo, ask yourself:

What's cool about this article?

How can I present the best parts of the article in a new way?

What's missing in this article?

What other topics can I plug into this one?

What are 5 new ideas I can bring to this content?

After about 20 or 30 articles, you'll begin to notice that the popular articles you used as a foundation for your own will completely disappear and you'll constantly be left with your own content that can buzz throughout your industry.

The internet is filled with rehashing of topics over and over which means your potential customers are itching for something new. Your goal in content production is to present new ideas and innovations that have never been spoken about. It takes a little bit of hard work and a lot of patience. However, if you can identify topics and content pieces that are buzzing moving through the internet like wild fire and you can consistently remake them into unique articles, you'll find yourself on a pot of gold that your competition wish they could find.

Remember that you get from articles what you put in. If you put in unique but explosive content, you'll be rewarded with regulars who love to visit your site. On the other hand, if you simply copy and paste what's already out there, you'll find yourself in the middle of an endless ocean of rehashed content.

Before you make every piece of content, ask yourself "what do I want my business to be remembered for?"

2. Headlines rule the world of first impressions.

A powerful headline separates a successful article from a total bust. Approximately 4 out of 5 of your readers will read the headline to your article. But sadly, only 1 out of 5 people will continue reading your post if you don't have a catchy headline.

After you put in the time and effort to make a great post, it's important to follow suit with a catchy hook that introduces it. Always take your time with headlines and pay close attention to which headlines spark engagement and interest.

Headlining is the backbone of all marketing and all of success in online business. If you can't catch your reader's attention in a simple sentence, then how in the world are you suppose to keep it for the rest of the article.

This book can't cover the power of headlines, but we can steer you in the right direction if you want to learn more.

Here are 3 fantastic links that will teach you more about writing explosive headlines.

https://marketingrebelclub.com/blog/john-carlton-perfect-headlines/

https://www.quicksprout.com/the-definitive-guide-to-copywriting-chapter-3/

http://www.businesswomenexperts.com/5-proven-headline-formulas-that-sell-like-crazy/

The important lesson presented inside succeeding in online business is to take your time with headlines. They'll teach you how to present your content, what the market cares about and ultimately how to sell you products in the long run.

3. Make sure you content can be applied.

The best content ever given to your potential customers comes through writing specific actions that can be taken to solve specific solutions. No matter what topic you chose to be in, you'll find that your market has a couple of problems they need to address.

By framing your content in a manner that can spark an action, you'll make your content exponentially more powerful. Even if it's a simple link to a new app or how to make a delicious cup of coffee. By constantly providing actions that can polish off every single article, you'll spark a massive improvement inside of your sales pitches as well as your user engagement.

Even if you're writing about a new Harry Potter Remote Wand you can attach a link to where they can access it (this got almost a million facebook shares). You don't have to make money in every article you write, but you do have to practice the art of CTAs(call to actions.)

Over time, you'll discover that a lot of people know a lot about your topic, but they aren't exactly sure what steps to take so they can get there. By constantly supplying your readers with ways to apply what you're presenting, you'll provide them with assurance that they can succeed through taking action on the material they just went through.

4. Be sure to use links to experts inside of your articles.

When your online business starts to pick up, you'll see that thousands of people will ready what your producing. Now imagine what would happen if your information turned out to be wrong and you faced whiplash from the info. This could completely diminish your reputation and you could loose all of your readers and have to start again from scratch.

Therefore, ensure that your information can at least be back checked by your readers. You don't have to always use a link, but if people ask questions, let them know where you found your info. This will allow you from facing fierce pushback for your content.

When you consistently give people credit for their ideas, statistics and innovations you'll be able to build your authority in the market through allowing your readers to understand the information arsenal you have under your belt.

Remember that you chose a business that you're passionate about so every new article you write should be fun. If it's not, make it enjoyable and twist topics in ways that you have a blast producing. Over time, you'll become an authority in the market and you'll even be able to use your generous linking as you begin trying to increase your traffic.

But more on that later. For now, simply remember that content accuracy builds faith in your visitors.

5. Always try to engage your readers.

Every article you create needs to spark contemplation while stirring up engagement. Without stimulating your audience, you'll begin to realize you have a hard time building your viewership. Therefor, the only way to get your readers to engage is through sparking that engagement. Makes sense right?

Here's a few ways for to spark engagement.

1.   Finish your content with a provoking question:

Questions don't mean you have to leave your post through the Soap Opera Method. Leaving readers with questions like "What do you think happened to Babylon?" after you present theories about why the civilization mysteriously vanished. Or if you're in entertainment you can ask readers "what are the top 3 animated movies released in 2016?" after you write a list of animated movies released in 2016.

2.   After your headline, find a way to spark an open ended intro that's fulfilled around the end of the content. This will spark your readers to consume your content in its entirety which is possibly the most powerful

form of engagement you can acquire from regular readers.

3.   Spark the beginning of another article at the end of your current piece of content. For example, let's say someone is cruising through an article about the top 5 guitar picks. You can then lead into how much more important guitar strings are in the feel and tone of playing music and ask readers to sign up to a newsletter so they can know when you'll release the next article. This is basically the soap opera sequencing that has been introduced above.

~Not every article has to have all three engagement strategies, but the more you utilize these engagement practices, the more you'll learn about the importance of engagement across your viewership. Have fun with these posts and try to get to know your readers. This will further spark engagement inside of your community.

6. Become a pro at telling stories.
It would be pretty crazy to find even 15% of a market that didn't like stories. Think about it, whether your visitors are reading, watching or simply listening, they inevitably enjoy

consuming information. This means that if stories are built into to your content, you'll stimulate imagination and excitement inside of your readers.

Stories have been embedded inside of civilization since the birth of language and things haven't changed for millenniums. It's theorized that stories improve engagement heavily, but the fact of the matter is that comments and scrolling throughout your websites will boost your rankings in Google. If you do something that will help your rankings on the search engines, it means you're on the right track. This is because search is designed for the users and no one else.

7. Add in an image and a video into every article.

People love pictures and video and it's crucial to understand that it's impossible to decrease consumption through adding in content that stimulates more of your viewership's senses. People do love reading, but by adding in new ways to present your content will allow you to build a broader range of audience. Some people don't like movies and some people don't like novels. But everyone likes a story and it's up to you to address every avenue of consumption.

Further guides on writing great content:

https://www.youtube.com/watch?v=MbS4Xg1wgUw

https://blog.kissmetrics.com/analytics-in-customer-engagement/

https://blog.hubspot.com/marketing/visual-content-marketing-strategy#sm.001s0pdpn15ypdf2qz612t5a580e9

https://blog.kissmetrics.com/emotional-targeting-converts-more-leads/

How often you produce content will determine whether you succeed of fail.

Kissmetrics has discovered that there's a direct correlation between how many posts you generate every day and how much traffic you'll ultimately generate over time. Starting an online business is a huge commitment because of the amount of posts you have to generate throughout the day. As a minimum, you should be generating an article a day but the more articles you can produce a day, the more viewers you'll average for every post and the quicker you'll be able to build your business.

Finding Free Pictures to Add To Your Content:

Filling up your website with pictures use to cost thousands of dollars, but over the past couple of years, sites have found a legal way to use other businesses' pictures through crediting them.

Here are 5 amazing websites that will allow you to develop successful posts and boost your user engagement.

1. Twitter
   https://support.twitter.com/articles/2016955 9
2. Pinterest
   https://developers.pinterest.com/tools/widget-builder/?
3. Tumblr
   http://embed.ly/provider/tumblr
4. Flickr

http://blog.flickr.net/en/2013/12/18/flickr-web-embeds/

5. Instagram
https://www.instagram.com/developer/embedding/

Or you can simply create an infographic with your content.

Creating Videos For Your Content:

Creating videos for your content is a perfect way to increase exposure for your content over a period of time. There are a couple of fun ways you can do this, so we'll break them down briefly below.

1. Make a slide presentation of your article.
2. Talk about your article in a video of yourself.
3. Create an animated video.
4. Hire someone to create a video for you on Fiverr.

You don't have to create videos right away as your launching your website, but the quicker you get your videos on youtube and the quicker you embed them onto your website, the quicker you'll increase your opportunities for exposure inside of your business.

Using this chapter as a foundation for your content creation, you'll put yourself in position to succeed inside of your online business. If done right, content is king. If done wrong, all of your hard work could be for not. When your building your website and your traffic pay special attention to developing your content.

And remember, start with 30 original posts to get yourself started on inside of your industry. After you get your first 30 pages of content set up, you can begin your journey

Chapter 4: Turning Content into Profits and Dollars

Now that you have a nice foundation of content laid out in front of you, it's time to begin to distribute it to monetize you business and to acquire traffic.

The first step inside of this set up comes through choosing what content you'd like to package as an opt-in. Opt-ins are the exchange of free information for emails and is the back bone of every business.

In order to do this, you need to acquire an autoresponder system.

The best autoresponders are:

http://www.aweber.com/

https://mailchimp.com

https://www.campaigner.com/

https://www.getresponse.com/

You can try all of these out on a free trial so don't hesitate to jump in. Having an autoresponder will give you access to one time visitors for years if you take great care of them.

Ways you can present an opt-in:

You can present your opt-in in 3 major ways:

1.   You can offer a free document like "10 hacks to double your traffic"

2.   You can offer a free course like "Double your productivity in 7 days."

3.   Or you can offer a free newsletter like "Ranting Writers."

No matter what you choose to offer, make sure that it's jam packed with great and useful information and that it will change the life of your visitor. Down the road, you'll begin to monetize your business and your email list will play a crucial role in your consistent income.

Here are 5 guidelines to creating a successful opt-in.

1. Be Specific

When you're going to acquire an email from your visitor try to be as specific as possible when you're creating your opt-in. This will allow you to convert on a specific topic and will make it easier to sell a related product inside of your email marketing. Never be broad and vague with your opt-ins.

2. Give them a silver bullet.

Think of a nice silver bullet that you're market's into. What topics were really big and what was everyone buzzing about? It's probably best to think of a simple and effective solution for that topic so you can generate a higher number of opt-ins from the same number of viewers. New online businesses often make the mistake of giving out tons of free little gits in exchange for an email. However, if you can simply blow your readers away with a great solution to a huge problem, you'll find yourself wit some excited subscribers every month.

4. Your opt-in has to quickly fill the needs of your customer.

When a customer gives you permission to send them emails, they're going to want to have a wonderful feeling of "instant" gratification after they exchange some private information to contact you. Even if you have a free course, the first day of your series has to be a home run for your new subscribers. Every opt-in that you ever create should be a quick read and quickly solve a big problem for your reader. This will give you a huge competitive edge as you recommend premium products to your email subscribers down the line.

5. It should be worth a lot.

Just because you're giving away free content doesn't mean that your content should have a free quality to it. Your opt-in page should feel like Black Friday for your customers. When they get a hold of it, they should be blown away that they got this content for free. The bigger your price tag is for your opt-in, the more impressed your new readers will be and the more trust they will have when you recommend buying things.

After you develop a nice opt-in for your viewers, it's time to find a product you can sell at the back end of your first email marketing campaign.

Don't move on to the next step until you have your autoresponder set up and you're opt-in page is live!

Although you'll probably want to sell you own products down the road, selling other people's products will help you generate income within the first couple of months of starting your business and that's ultimately what you want.

Select a product that's closely related to your free opt-in and try to sell it through a simple email marketing series.

Selecting the product you're going to try to sell.

There are a couple of networks you can use to sell your products through. All of theses presented are reputable sites with proven track records.

I. http://www.clickbank.com/

II. http://marketing.rakuten.com/affiliate-marketing

III. http://shareasale.com/

IV. http://www.avangate.com/affiliates/

V. https://affiliate-program.amazon.com/

These websites all allow you to select from a great portfolio of products to generate your first sales and provide the benchmark for affiliate marketing. Have fun in selecting what you're going to sell!

YOUR FIRST EMAIL CAMPAIGN:

There's no easy way to briefly dive into email marketing. Luckily, there is a great resource that will give you a firm foundation on monetizing your email marketing efforts.

http://www.digitalmarketer.com/email-marketing-machine/

This article feels like it goes on forever(and ever) and it's filled with tons of information about different aspects of running online business. However, the beginning of the page has exactly what you need and is the perfect introduction on how you should develop your initial email marketing campaign.

Enjoy and after you set up your first autoresponder campaign, you can move on to the next step to generate some initial traffic for your business!

This book is designed to maximize your efforts and to streamline starting an online business. If you jump around without completing actions, you'll find yourself having to put in extra work because you'll be missing some essential ingredients it takes to get a website ready for a first wave of sales. Remember that anyone can do the steps required throughout this book. It's up to you to take these simple actions so you can get your online business off the ground and have a great 2017.

Chapter 4:

Distributing

Your

Content.

Now that you've put in a ton of hard work to set up your business, it's time to advertise your business.

No matter what happens, it's important to make sure you have at least one article available in each category that's open on your website.

And if you are worried about how many articles you have available, you can do a small personalize preview of 50-100 articles that link to other websites. That way, you can show off your knowledge while minimizing the amount of time you spend writing your articles.

All you have to do to pull this trick off is write 100 words about your favorite articles and then link them at the end of your description. This will allow you to disguise how new you are to your business and it'll even help generate authorities linking to your really cool descriptions on their content over time!

Now, this next step dives into the initial traffic phase inside of your new business. The second book in this series will give you a blueprint to develop free traffic through tapping into social media. But for now, it's time for some pay off for all the hard work you've done.

This chapter is designed to take some of the content you've already produced and to put it in the hands of viewers around the world. Things may start off a little bit slow, but after some patience, your business will take off and you'll have some profits in your pocket!

When you have some good content on your hands, there are a couple of ways you can use it to your advantage.

1. Contact already successful online businesses.

The first crazy successful way to capitalize on content you have is through trying to get your articles on other websites. This does 2 major things for your business.

1.   It will allow you to reach tons of new readers through writing only one piece of content.

2.   It gives you a nice position as an authority figure inside of your market.

Here's a nice way to start getting your foot into the door with other businesses inside of your market.

1.   **Simply guest post**
Guest posting is catching on fire over the past couple years. Thousands of business owners have swept into the scene through simply writing on other people's websites so they can promote their business to new readers from around the world. It may take a little bit of time to develop a nice from of

2.   **Upgrade some of your content once a month and use it to guest post**

Before long, you're going to have an insane number of articles, infographics, and videos on your website. If you go back and read through your published content once a month, you'll begin to develop some breakthroughs in sparking new ideas, new articles and new content for your business.

3.   **Don't be afraid to get shut down, but do make an effort to be sincere.**

4.   When you contact businesses to guest post some of your content, keep in mind that there could be dozens of people asking to write on their website every week. This is why it's important to put in a little bit of groundwork you can use to your advantage. When you approach to write on someone's blog, don't give them trash. Give them the best thing you've got and actually know what's on their blog. Complement them on a couple of posts and let them know about the impact that they've made in your life. Your goal is to truly connect to potential business friends and to give them the attention they deserve.

5.   **Give the people you email some time to respond.**

Most businesses are extremely busy throughout the week and it may take a while to get back to you and you might ultimately never end up with a response at all. Don't take it personally. Some people are just flooded with things to do and they genuinely don't have time to respond back. You'll probably find yourself in this position in a couple years. So don't get worried about whether or not you're good enough. Just keep plugging away!

2. Share published content to your social media accounts

Social media is an incredible opportunity for you to showcase your business. You should have already made a facebook and a twitter account. If you've chosen to develop some videos to accompany it, you've probably included a youtube. Luckily, using these 3 platforms allows us to develop a nice following. Every active user has about a 100 friends. This means that you content could reach millions of people over the span of dozens of posts. That probably won't happen, but the opportunity to make splashes inside for your business are unmatched when it comes to free exposure.

3. Send your content through to your subscribers.

As your email list rises, you'll find that you'll get a nice boost to the content you produce if you promote it to your email list. It's one of the best platforms to reach an active part of your viewership. The quicker you can get buzz through every piece of content, the quicker you can increase the number of readers that visit your website .

And we share each blog post more than once, according to a promotion schedule that spreads the promotion across a week or more (often stretching out to a month).

4. Mention influencers inside of your posts and then let them know.

If you play your cards right, mentioning some key players inside of your market can generate a huge readership to your website. If you followed the guidelines to produce your content, you'll probably have a list of people you linked to inside of your website pages. You can send them a friendly email letting them know how much you like their content and you can ask for advice on how to improve your content. After you develop a conversation with them, feel free to ask them about a new article you wrote and see if they'd like to have it on their website for free! It's a more advanced form of guest posting and you might even be able to get some free exposure if the expert you featured in your content shares it with his email subscribers.

Worst case, you'll get some nice advice and you'll learn some cool tricks to expand your business!

5. Submit the content to communities

There are tons of communities out there that are alive with readers but they tend to change with every market.

By looking and doing some research, you'll find that you can present some of your fresh content to thousands of new readers and you'll get some great exposure in the long run.

A couple of great places to start are reddit, feedly, stumbleupon, triberr, scoop.it and engage.

You'll find that if you consistently engage inside of these websites you'll become loaded with tons of new ideas for content and you'll eventually make a splash and bring some readers back to your website.

When you're developing your business, it's important to use as many of these strategies as you can to develop some income.

And don't join any community just to share what you've written. Engage in other people's content, join the conversation and actually become a member of what business you're launching.

If you follow the simple actions inside of this book, you're going to have a wonderful 2017. But don't delay and don't look for more information before you get started.

Start taking action and if you have questions along the way, feel free to research solutions to the problems that arise and then get back to the actions inside of this book.

You'll find that there are thousands of ways to start a business, but this book lays out a very smooth and easy approach to getting started.

There's always something to improve on in the world of business, but if you set out to become an expert before you get started, you'll never take action and generate an income through one of your passions. Most importantly, have fun in your journey and let us know if you have any questions or if you have any feedback.

Enjoy!

BONUS

FREE TRAFFIC MARKETING REPORT
<u>ACCESS NOW</u>:
http://successtornado.com/Free
-Traffic-Marketing.pdf